4-Chord Songbook
Christmas Songs

CU00703919

This publication is not authorised for sale in the United States of America and/or Canada

WISE PUBLICATIONS
part of The Music Sales Group

London / New York / Paris / Sydney / Copenhagen / Berlin / Madrid / Tokyo

This *4-Chord Songbook* allows even beginner guitarists to play and enjoy your favourite hits. The songs have been specially arranged so that only 4 chords are needed to play all of the songs in the book.

The *4-Chord Songbook* doesn't use music notation. Throughout the book chord boxes are printed at the head of each song; the chord changes are shown above the lyrics. It's left to you, the guitarist, to decide on a strum pattern or picking pattern.

Some of the arrangements indicate that a capo should be used at a particular fret. This is to match the song to the key of the original recording so that you can play along; otherwise the capo is not needed for playing on your own. However, if the pitch of the vocal line is not comfortable for singing (if it is pitched too high or too low) you may wish to use a capo anyway; placing the capo behind a suitable fret will change the key of the song without learning any new chords.

Whatever you do, this *4-Chord Songbook* guarantees hours of enjoyment for guitarists of all levels, as well as providing a fine basis for building a strong repertoire.

Published by
Wise Publications
14-15 Berners Street, London W1T 3LJ, UK.

Exclusive Distributors:
Music Sales Limited
Distribution Centre, Newmarket Road, Bury St Edmunds, Suffolk IP33 3YB, UK.
Music Sales Pty Limited
20 Resolution Drive, Caringbah, NSW 2229, Australia.

Order No. AM995247
ISBN 978-1-84772-712-1
This book © Copyright 2008 Wise Publications,
a division of Music Sales Limited.

Unauthorised reproduction of any part of this publication by
any means including photocopying is an infringement of copyright.

Edited by Sam Harrop.
Printed in the EU.

www.musicsales.com

Your Guarantee of Quality

As publishers, we strive to produce every book to the highest commercial standards.

The music has been freshly engraved and the book has been carefully designed to minimise awkward page turns and to make playing from it a real pleasure.

Particular care has been given to specifying acid-free, neutral-sized paper made from pulps which have not been elemental chlorine bleached.

This pulp is from farmed sustainable forests and was produced with special regard for the environment.

Throughout, the printing and binding have been planned to ensure a sturdy, attractive publication which should give years of enjoyment.

If your copy fails to meet our high standards, please inform us and we will gladly replace it.

Relative Tuning

The guitar can be tuned with the aid of pitch pipes or dedicated electronic guitar tuners which are available through your local music dealer. If you do not have a tuning device, you can use relative tuning. Estimate the pitch of the 6th string as near as possible to E or at least a comfortable pitch (not too high, as you might break other strings in tuning up). Then, while checking the various positions on the diagram, place a finger from your left hand on the:

5th fret of the E or 6th string and **tune the open A** (or 5th string) to the note (A)

5th fret of the A or 5th string and **tune the open D** (or 4th string) to the note (D)

5th fret of the D or 4th string and **tune the open G** (or 3rd string) to the note (G)

4th fret of the G or 3rd string and **tune the open B** (or 2nd string) to the note (B)

5th fret of the B or 2nd string and **tune the open E** (or 1st string) to the note (E)

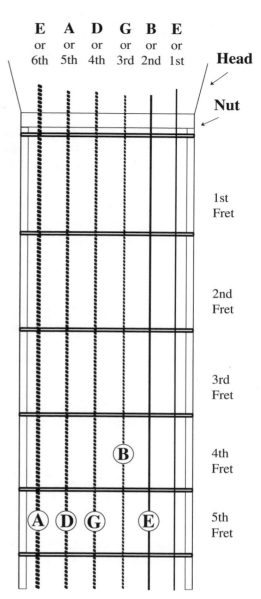

Reading Chord Boxes

Chord boxes are diagrams of the guitar neck viewed head upwards, face on as illustrated. The top horizontal line is the nut, unless a higher fret number is indicated, the others are the frets.

The vertical lines are the strings, starting from E (or 6th) on the left to E (or 1st) on the right.

The black dots indicate where to place your fingers.

Strings marked with an O are played open, not fretted. Strings marked with an X should not be played.

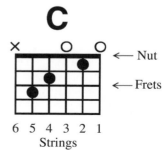

As With Gladness Men Of Old

Words by William Chatterton Dix
Music by Conrad Kocher

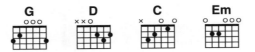

Verse 1

```
G  D        G  C  D G
```
As with glad - ness men of old

```
C     G      C  G  D  G
```
Did the guid - ing star be - hold;

```
G  D        G  C   D G
```
As with joy they hailed its light,

```
C      G     C  G    D  G
```
Leading on - ward beam - ing bright.

```
G  D  Em   D         G
```
So, most gracious Lord, may we

```
C    G     C G D G
```
Ever - more be led by Thee.

Verse 2

```
(G) D        G C   D  G
```
As with joy - ful steps they sped,

```
C     G C  G    D G
```
Saviour, to Thy low - ly bed,

```
      D G      C  D G
```
There to bend the knee be - fore

```
C         G     C  G   D G
```
Thee whom heaven and earth a - dore.

```
     D  Em   D    G
```
So may we with willing feet

```
C   G    C  G   D  G
```
Ever seek Thy mer - cy - seat.
```

© Copyright 2008 Dorsey Brothers Music Limited.
All Rights Reserved. International Copyright Secured.
```

Verse 3

(G) D   G   C   D   G
As they offered gifts most rare

C   G   C G D   G
At thy cra - dle rude and bare,

**   D   G   C   D G**
So may we with ho - ly joy,

C   G C   G   D G
Pure, and free from sin's al - loy,

**   D   Em   D   G**
All our costliest treasures bring,

C   G   C G   D   G
Christ to Thee our hea - venly King.

Verse 4

(G)   D G   C   D G
Ho - ly Jesus, ev - 'ry day

C   G C G   D   G
Keep us in the nar - row way:

**   D   G   C   D   G**
And, when earthly things are past

C   G   C   G   D G
Bring our ran - somed souls at last,

**   D   Em   D   G**
Where they need no soul to guide,

C   G   C G   D G
Where no clouds Thy glo - ry hide.

Verse 5

(G) D   G   C   D G
In the heavenly coun - try bright

C   G C   G D G
Need they no cre - a - ted light;

**   D G   C   D G**
Thou its light, its joy, its crown,

C   G   C   G   D G
Thou its sun, which goes not down.

**   D   Em D   G**
There for ever may we sing

C   G   C   G D G
Halle - lu - jahs to our King.

The Boar's Head Carol

Traditional

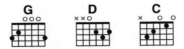

Verse 1

N.C.
The boar's head in hand bear I,

Bedecked with bays and rosemary;

And I pray you my masters, be merry,

Quo testis in convivio:

Chorus 1

G   D   G   D
Caput apri defe - ro,
C   G   D G
Reddens laudes Dom - i - no.

© Copyright 2008 Dorsey Brothers Music Limited.
All Rights Reserved. International Copyright Secured.

Verse 2

N.C.
The boar's head, as I understand

Is the rarest dish in all this land,

Which thus bedecked with a gay garland,

Let us *servire cantico:*

Chorus 2

G　　　**D**　**G**　　**D**
Caput apri defe - ro,
C　　　　　**G**　　**D G**
Reddens laudes Dom - i - no.

Verse 3

N.C.
Our steward hath provided this,

In honour of the King of bliss,

Which on this day to be served is,

In Reginensi atrio:

Chorus 3

G　　　**D**　**G**　　**D**
Caput apri defe - ro,
C　　　　　**G**　　**D G**
Reddens laudes Dom - i - no.

Ding Dong Merrily On High

Words by George Woodward
Music: Traditional

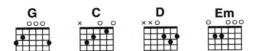

Verse 1

    G   C   D
Ding dong! Merrily on high,

     C   D   G
In heav'n the bells are ringing.

     C   D
Ding dong! Verily the sky,

     C   D   G
Is riv'n with angel singing.

Refrain 1

| G | Em | C | D | G | Em | D |
Glo - - - - - - - - - - - - - - - ria

    C   D   G
Ho - sanna in ex - celsis!

Verse 2

G   C   D
E'en so here below, be - low,

    C   D   G
Let steeple bells be swungen,

    C   D
And io, io, io,

    C   D   G
By priest and people sungen.

© Copyright 2008 Dorsey Brothers Music Limited.
All Rights Reserved. International Copyright Secured.

Refrain 2

| G | Em | C | D | G | Em | D |

Glo - - - - - - - - - - - - - - - - - ria

C   D   G

Ho - sanna in ex - celsis!

Verse 3

G   C   D

Pray you dutifully prime,

C   D   G

Your matin chime, ye ringers;

C   D

May you beautifully rhyme

C   D   G

Your evetime song, ye singers.

Refrain 3

| G | Em | C | D | G | Em | D |

Glo - - - - - - - - - - - - - - - - - ria

C   D   G

Ho - sanna in ex - celsis!

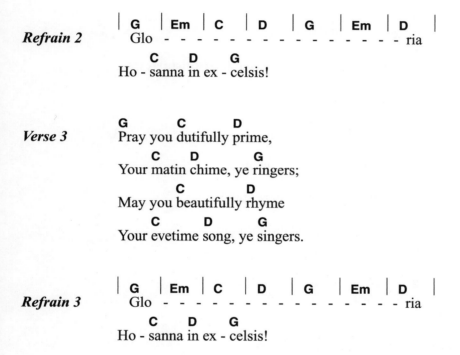

Early Christmas Morning

Words & Music by
Cyndi Lauper & Jan Pulsford

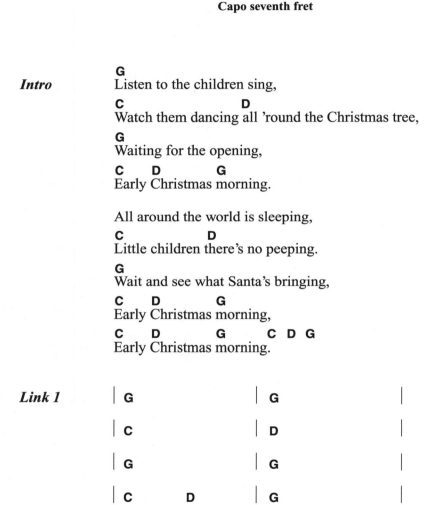

Capo seventh fret

Intro

G
Listen to the children sing,
C   **D**
Watch them dancing all 'round the Christmas tree,
G
Waiting for the opening,
C **D** **G**
Early Christmas morning.

All around the world is sleeping,
C   **D**
Little children there's no peeping.
G
Wait and see what Santa's bringing,
C **D** **G**
Early Christmas morning,
C **D** **G** **C D G**
Early Christmas morning.

Link 1 | G | G |

       | C | D |

       | G | G |

       | C D | G |

© Copyright 1996 Rellla Music Corporation/Tenja Music, USA.
Rondor Music (London) Limited (50%)/
Sony/ATV Music Publishing (UK) Limited (50%).
All Rights Reserved. International Copyright Secured.

Verse 1

G
Listen to the children sing,

C   **D**
Watch them dancing all 'round the Christmas tree,

G
Waiting for the opening,

C   **D**   **G**
Early Christmas morning.

Chorus 1

(G)
All around the world is sleeping,

C   **D**
Little children there's no peeping.

G
Wait and see what Santa's bringing,

C   **D**   **G**
Early Christmas morning,

C   **D**   **G**   **C   D**
Early Christmas morning.

Verse 2

G
Icicles and breakfast cakes,

C   **D**
Friends and family we will celebrate,

G
Sounds that joy and laughter make,

C   **D**   **G**
Early Christmas morning.

Chorus 2

(G)
All around and far off places,

C   **D**
Angels waken smiling faces.

G
Wrapping us with love and graces,

C   **D**   **G**
Early Christmas morning,

C   **D**   **G**
Early Christmas morning,

C   **D**
Early Christmas.

Link 2

G			G		
C			D		
G			G		
C	D		G		

Verse 3

G
Listen to the children sing,

                     D
Watch them dancing all 'round the Christmas tree,

G
Waiting for the opening,

C   D   G
Early Christmas morning.

Chorus 3

(G)
All around the world is sleeping,

C   D
Little children there's no peeping.

G
Wait and see what Santa's bringing,

   C   D   G
‖: Early Christmas morning,

C   D   G
Early Christmas morning. :‖ *repeat ad lib. to fade*

Feliz Navidad

Words & Music by
José Feliciano

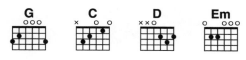

Capo seventh fret

Intro | G | C | D | G | G | C | D | G ||

Verse 1
          C   D   G
Feliz navi - dad,   feliz navi - dad,
          C   D   G
Feliz navi - dad, prospero año y felici - dad.
          C   D   G
Feliz navi - dad,   feliz navi - dad,
          C   D   G
Feliz navi - dad, prospero año y felici - dad.

Chorus 1
                           C   D
‖: I wanna wish you a merry Christmas,
                      G   Em
I wanna wish you a merry Christmas,
                      C
I wanna wish you a merry Christmas,
         D   G
From the bottom of my heart. :‖

Verse 2   As Verse 1

Chorus 2   As Chorus 1

Verse 3   As Verse 1

Chorus 3   As Chorus 1

Coda
          C   D   G
Feliz navi - dad,   feliz navi - dad,
          C   D   G
Feliz navi - dad, prospero año y felici - dad.

© Copyright 1970 J & H Publishing Company, USA.
Dejamus Limited.
All Rights Reserved. International Copyright Secured.

Everything's Gonna Be Cool This Christmas

Words & Music by
Mark Everett

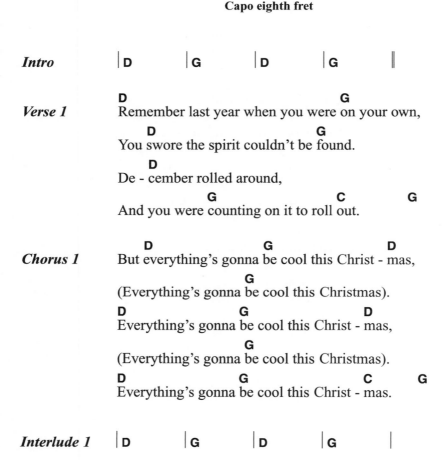

D   **G**   **C**

Capo eighth fret

Intro | D | G | D | G   ‖

Verse 1
      D   **G**
Remember last year when you were on your own,
      D   **G**
You swore the spirit couldn't be found.
      D
De - cember rolled around,
          G   **C**   **G**
And you were counting on it to roll out.

Chorus 1
         D   **G**   **D**
But everything's gonna be cool this Christ - mas,
            G
(Everything's gonna be cool this Christmas).
D   **G**   **D**
Everything's gonna be cool this Christ - mas,
            G
(Everything's gonna be cool this Christmas).
D   **G**   **C**   **G**
Everything's gonna be cool this Christ - mas.

Interlude 1 | D | G | D | G |

© Copyright 1998 Vitamin E Music/PolyGram International Publishing Incorporated, USA.
Universal Music Publishing Limited.
All rights in Germany administered by Universal Music Publ. GmbH.
All Rights Reserved. International Copyright Secured.

Verse 2

          D   G
Well everybody's looking for you down at the house,

          D   G
The tree is looking so in - spired.

              D   G
There's a yuletide groove waiting for you to move,

                 C   G
Oh, come and throw another log on the fire.

Chorus 2   As Chorus 1

Interlude 2 | D | G | D |

                    D   G
                    Baby Jesus, born to rock.

Instrumental | C | G | C | G | C | G || D | G | D | G |

Middle

              D
As days go by,

                    G
The more that we need friends,

               D   G
And the harder they are to find.

            D   G
If I could have a friend like you in my life,

            C   G
Then I guess I'd be doing just fine.

Chorus 3   As Chorus 1

Outro | C | G | C | G |

             | C | G | C | G |

             | D | G | D | G |

             | D | G | D | G |

             | D ||

Fairytale Of New York

Words & Music by
Shane MacGowan & Jem Finer

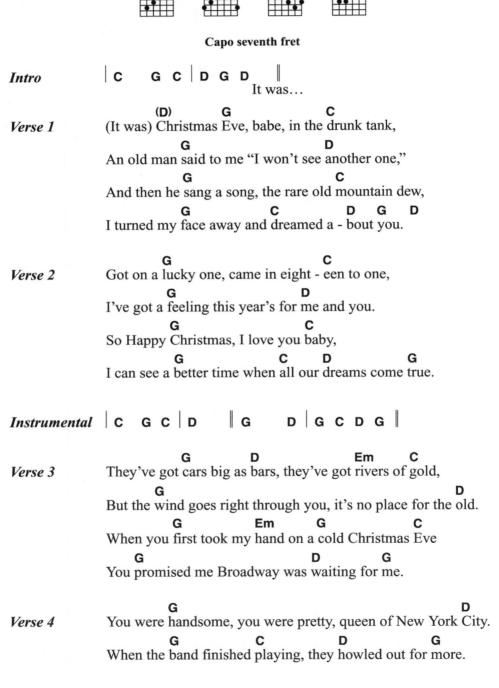

Capo seventh fret

Intro

|C   G C |D G D | It was…

Verse 1

       (D)   **G**   **C**
(It was) Christmas Eve, babe, in the drunk tank,
     G   **D**
An old man said to me "I won't see another one,"
      G   **C**
And then he sang a song, the rare old mountain dew,
    G   **C**   **D G   D**
I turned my face away and dreamed a - bout you.

Verse 2

     G   **C**
Got on a lucky one, came in eight - een to one,
     G   **D**
I've got a feeling this year's for me and you.
     G   **C**
So Happy Christmas, I love you baby,
     G   **C** **D**   **G**
I can see a better time when all our dreams come true.

Instrumental |C   G C |D ‖G   D |G C D G‖

Verse 3

     G   **D**   **Em** **C**
They've got cars big as bars, they've got rivers of gold,
     G   **D**
But the wind goes right through you, it's no place for the old.
     G   **Em** **G**   **C**
When you first took my hand on a cold Christmas Eve
     G   **D**   **G**
You promised me Broadway was waiting for me.

Verse 4

     G   **D**
You were handsome, you were pretty, queen of New York City.
     G   **C**   **D**   **G**
When the band finished playing, they howled out for more.

© Copyright 1987 Perfect Songs Limited (50%)/Universal Music Publishing MGB Limited (50%)
(administered in Germany by Musik Edition Discoton GmbH).
All Rights Reserved. International Copyright Secured.

G   D
Sin - atra was swinging, all the drunks they were singing,
                    G   C   D   G
We kissed on a corner then danced through the night.

Chorus 1
                            C   Em   D   G   Em
And the boys from the NYPD   choir were singin' 'Galway Bay',
                            G   C   D
And the bells were ringin' out for Christmas (Day.)

Link 1 | G D Em C | G   D | G Em G C | G   D G ‖
                    Day.

Verse 5
                            G   D
You're a bum, you're a punk, you're an old slut on a junk,
                            G   C   D   G
Lying there almost dead on a drip in that bed.
                            G   D
You scumbag, you maggot, you cheap lousy faggot,
                            G   C   D   G
Happy Christmas your arse, I pray God it's our last.

Chorus 2   As Chorus 1

Link 2 | G | C | G   C | D G D   ‖
                    Day.   I could have…

Verse 6
                            G   C
(I could have) been someone, well so could anyone.
                            G   D
You took my dreams from me when I first found you.
                            G   C
I kept them with me, babe, I put them with my own,
                            G   C   D   G
I can't make it all alone, I've built my dreams a - round you.

Chorus 3
                            C   Em   D   G   Em
And the boys from the NYPD   choir were singin' 'Galway Bay',
                            N.C.
And the bells were ringin' out for Christmas (Day.)

Outro   ‖: G | C | G   C | D G D :‖ *Repeat to fade*
                    Day.

17

Go Tell It On The Mountain

Traditional

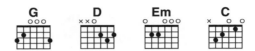

Chorus 1

G
Go, tell it on the mountain,
D   **G**
Over the hills and ev'rywhere.

Go, tell it on the mountain
     D   **G**
That Jesus Christ is born.

Verse 1

(G)
When I was first a learner,
    D   **G**
I sought both night and day.
          Em
I asked the Lord to help me,
   C   **D**
And he showed me the way.

Chorus 2

G
Go, tell it on the mountain,
D   **G**
Over the hills and ev'rywhere.

Go, tell it on the mountain
     D   **G**
That Jesus Christ is born.

Verse 2

(G)
Then he made me a watchman
    D   **G**
Up - on the city wall,
        Em
And if I am a Christian,
   C   **D**
I am the least of all.

© Copyright 2008 Dorsey Brothers Music Limited.
All Rights Reserved. International Copyright Secured.

Chorus 3

G
Go, tell it on the mountain,
D   G
Over the hills and ev'rywhere.

Go, tell it on the mountain
      D   G
That Jesus Christ is born.

Verse 3

(G)
While shepherds kept their watching
      D   G
O'er wand'ring flocks by night;
              Em
Behold from out the heavens
      C   D
There shone a holy light.

Chorus 4

G
Go, tell it on the mountain,
D   G
Over the hills and ev'rywhere.

Go, tell it on the mountain
      D   G
That Jesus Christ is born.

Verse 4

(G)
And lo! When they had seen it,
      D   G
They all bowed down and prayed;
              Em
Then travelled on to - gether,
     C   D
To where the babe was laid.

Chorus 5

G
Go, tell it on the mountain,
D   G
Over the hills and ev'rywhere.

Go, tell it on the mountain
      D   G
That Jesus Christ is born.

Good King Wenceslas

Words by J.M. Neale
Music: Traditional

G   Em   D   C

Verse 1

G   Em   D   G   C   D
Good King Wen - ces - las looked out,

C   G   C   D   G
On the feast of Stephen,

       Em   D   G   C   D
When the snow lay round a - bout,

C   G   C   D   G
Deep and crisp and even;

       C G   D   G   D   Em
Bright - ly shone the moon that night,

C   G   C   D   G
Though the frost was cruel,

       C   D   Em   D
When a poor man came in sight,

G   C   G   D   Em C   G
Gath' - ring win - ter fu - el.

Verse 2

      (G)   Em   D   G   C D
"Hither, page and stand by me,

C   G   C   D   G
If thou know'st it, telling.

       Em   D   G   C D
Yonder peas - ant who is he?

C   G   C   D   G
Where, and what his dwelling?"

       C G   D G   D   Em
"Sire, he lives a   good league hence,

C   G   C   D   G
Un - der - neath the mountain;

       C   D   Em   D
Right a - gainst the forest fence,

G   C   G   D   Em   C   G
By Saint Ag - nes fount - tain."

© Copyright 2008 Dorsey Brothers Music Limited.
All Rights Reserved. International Copyright Secured.

Verse 3

(G)   **Em**   **D**   **G**   **C**   **D**
"Bring me flesh and bring me wine,

C   **G**   **C**   **D**   **G**
Bring me pine logs hither;

       Em   **D**   **G**   **C**   **D**
Thou and I   will see him dine,

C   **G**   **C**   **D**   **G**
When we bear them hither."

        C   **G**   **D**   **G**   **D**   **Em**
Page and mon - arch forth they went,

C   **G**   **C**   **D**   **G**
Forth they went to - gether;

         C   **D**   **Em**   **D**
Through the rude wind's wild la - ment

G   **C**   **G**   **D** **Em**   **C**   **G**
And the bit - ter weath   -   er.

Verse 4

(G)   **Em**   **D**   **G**   **C**   **D**
"Sire, the night is dar - ker now,

C   **G**   **C**   **D**   **G**
And the wind blows stronger;

       Em   **D** **G**   **C**   **D**
Fails my heart, I   know not how,

C **G**   **C**   **D** **G**
I   can go no longer."

        C   **G**   **D**   **G**   **D**   **Em**
"Mark my foot - steps, good my page!

C   **G**   **C** **D**   **G**
Tread thou in them boldly:

         C   **D**   **Em**   **D**
Thou shalt find the winter's rage

G   **C**   **G**   **D**   **Em**   **C G**
Freeze thy blood less cold   -   ly."

Verse 5

(G)   **Em**   **D**   **G**   **C D**
In his mas - ter's steps he trod,

C   **G**   **C**   **D**   **G**
Where the snow lay dinted;

       Em   **D**   **G**   **C D**
Heat was in   the ve - ry sod

C   **G**   **C**   **D**   **G**
Which the saint had printed.

        C   **G**   **D**   **G**   **D**   **Em**
There - fore, Chris - tian men, be sure,

C   **G** **C**   **D**   **G**
Wealth or rank pos - sessing,

       C   **D**   **Em**   **D**
Ye who now will bless the poor,

G   **C**   **G**   **D**   **Em**   **C G**
Shall your - selves find bless   -   ing.

The Holly And The Ivy

Traditional

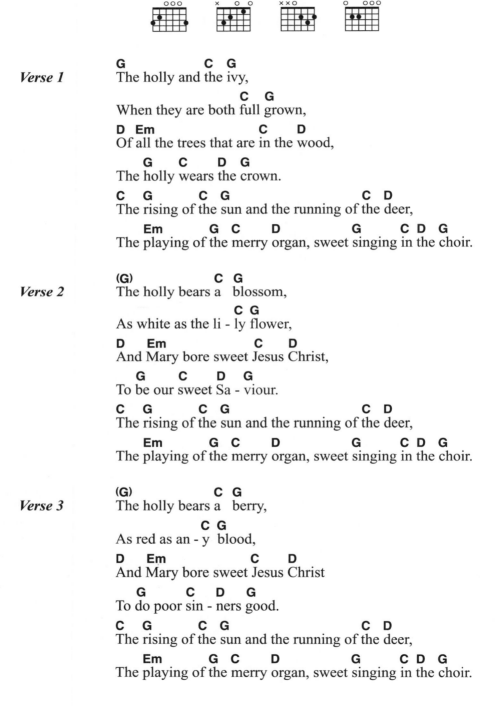

Verse 1

G   C G
The holly and the ivy,

       C G
When they are both full grown,

D Em   C D
Of all the trees that are in the wood,

  G C D G
The holly wears the crown.

C G   C G   C D
The rising of the sun and the running of the deer,

   Em   G C D   G C D G
The playing of the merry organ, sweet singing in the choir.

Verse 2

(G)   C G
The holly bears a blossom,

       C G
As white as the li - ly flower,

D Em   C D
And Mary bore sweet Jesus Christ,

  G C D G
To be our sweet Sa - viour.

C G   C G   C D
The rising of the sun and the running of the deer,

   Em   G C D   G C D G
The playing of the merry organ, sweet singing in the choir.

Verse 3

(G)   C G
The holly bears a berry,

    C G
As red as an - y blood,

D Em   C D
And Mary bore sweet Jesus Christ

  G C D G
To do poor sin - ners good.

C G   C G   C D
The rising of the sun and the running of the deer,

   Em   G C D   G C D G
The playing of the merry organ, sweet singing in the choir.

© Copyright 2008 Dorsey Brothers Music Limited.
All Rights Reserved. International Copyright Secured.

Verse 4

```
(G)              C  G
The holly bears a   prickle,
                 C  G
As sharp as an - y  thorn,
D   Em           C     D
And Mary bore sweet Jesus Christ
   G       C   D   G
On Christmas day in the morn.
C   G     C  G               C  D
The rising of the sun and the running of the deer,
      Em       G  C    D       G      C D G
The playing of the merry organ, sweet singing in the choir.
```

Verse 5

```
(G)              C  G
The holly bears a   bark,
                 C  G
As bitter as an - y  gall,
D   Em           C     D
And Mary bore sweet Jesus Christ
   G     C    D  G
For to re - deem us   all.
C   G     C  G               C  D
The rising of the sun and the running of the deer,
      Em       G  C    D       G      C D G
The playing of the merry organ, sweet singing in the choir.
```

Verse 6

```
(G)            C  G
The holly and the ivy,
                   C  G
When they are both full grown,
D   Em             C     D
Of all the trees that are in the wood,
    G   C    D  G
The holly bears the crown.
C   G     C  G               C  D
The rising of the sun and the running of the deer,
      Em       G  C    D       G      C D G
The playing of the merry organ, sweet singing in the choir.
```

I Saw Three Ships

Traditional

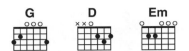

G   **D**   **Em**

Verse 1

G   D
I saw three ships come sailing in,
  Em   D
On Christmas day, on Christmas day;
G   D
I saw three ships come sailing in
  G   Em   D   G
On Christmas day in the morning.

Verse 2

     G   D
And what was in those ships all three,
  Em   D
On Christmas day, on Christmas day;
     G   D
And what was in those ships all three,
  G   Em   D   G
On Christmas day in the morning.

Verse 3

     G   D
The Virgin Mary and Christ were there,
  Em   D
On Christmas day, on Christmas day;
     G   D
The Virgin Mary and Christ were there,
  G   Em   D   G
On Christmas day in the morning.

Verse 4

     G   D
Pray, whither sailed those ships all three,
  Em   D
On Christmas day, on Christmas day?
     G   D
Pray, whither sailed those ships all three,
  G   Em   D   G
On Christmas day in the morning?

© Copyright 2008 Dorsey Brothers Music Limited.
All Rights Reserved. International Copyright Secured.

Verse 5

    G   **D**
O they sailed into Bethlehem,

      Em   **D**
On Christmas day, on Christmas day;

    G   **D**
O they sailed into Bethlehem,

    G   **Em**   **D**   **G**
On Christmas day in the morning.

Verse 6

     G   **D**
And all the bells on earth shall ring,

      Em   **D**
On Christmas day, on Christmas day;

     G   **D**
And all the bells on earth shall ring,

    G   **Em**   **D**   **G**
On Christmas day in the morning.

Verse 7

     G   **D**
And all the angels in heaven shall sing,

      Em   **D**
On Christmas day, on Christmas day;

     G   **D**
And all the angels in heaven shall sing,

    G   **Em**   **D**   **G**
On Christmas day in the morning.

Verse 8

     G   **D**
And all the souls on earth shall sing,

      Em   **D**
On Christmas day, on Christmas day;

     G   **D**
And all the souls on earth shall sing,

    G   **Em**   **D**   **G**
On Christmas day in the morning.

Verse 9

     G   **D**
Then let us all rejoice again,

      Em   **D**
On Christmas day, on Christmas day;

     G   **D**
Then let us all rejoice again,

    G   **Em**   **D**   **G**
On Christmas day in the morning.

In The Bleak Midwinter

Words by Christina Rossetti
Music by Gustav Holst

G   Em   C   D

Verse 1

G   **Em**
In the bleak mid - winter

C   **D**
Frosty wind made moan,

G   **Em**
Earth stood hard as iron,

C   **D**   **G**
Water like a stone.

C   **G**   **C**   **Em**
Snow had fal - len, snow on snow,

G   **C D**
Snow on snow.

G   **Em**
In the bleak mid - winter,

C   **D**   **G**
Long___ a - go.

Verse 2

    (G)   **Em**
Our God, heaven cannot hold Him

C   **D**
Nor earth sus - tain;

G   **Em**
Heaven and earth shall flee away

C   **D**   **G**
When He comes to reign:

C   **G**   **C**   **Em**
In the bleak mid - win - ter

   G   **C**   **D**
A stable place suf - ficed.

    G   **Em**
The Lord God Al - mighty

C D   **G**
Je - sus Christ.

© Copyright 2008 Dorsey Brothers Music Limited.
All Rights Reserved. International Copyright Secured.

Verse 3

      (G)   **Em**
E - nough for Him, whom Cherubim

C   **D**
Worship night and day,

  G   **Em**
A breastful of milk

      C   **D** **G**
And a manger - ful of hay;

      C   **G** **C**   **Em**
E - nough for Him, whom An - gels

G **C**   **D**
Fall down be - fore,

      G   **Em**
The ox and ass and camel

C   **D** **G**
Which a - dore.

Verse 4

(G)   **Em**
Angels and Arch - angels

C   **D**
May have gathered there,

G   **Em**
Cherubim and Seraphim

C   **D** **G**
Thronged __ the air:

      C **G** **C**   **Em**
But only his moth - er

G   **C**   **D**
In her maiden bliss,

G   **Em**
Worshipped the be - loved

C   **D** **G**
With a   kiss.

Verse 5

(G)   **Em**
What can I give Him,

C   **D**
Poor as I am?

G   **Em**
If I were a shepherd

C   **D**   **G**
I would bring a lamb;

C   **G** **C**   **Em**
If I were a wise man

G   **C**   **D**
I would do my part;

    G   **Em**
Yet what can I give Him,

C   **D** **G**
Give my heart.

Jingle Bells

Words & Music by
J.S. Pierpont

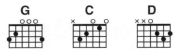

Verse 1

G
Dashing through the snow
               C
In a one-horse open sleigh,
           D
O'er the fields we go,
          G
Laughing all the way.

Bells on bobtail ring
         C
Making spirits bright.
           D
What fun it is to ride and sing
         G
A sleighing song to - night.

Chorus 1

(G)
Jingle bells, jingle bells,
    C   **G**
Jingle all the way.
C   **G**
Oh, what fun it is to ride
    D
In a one-horse open sleigh.
    G
Oh, jingle bells, jingle bells,
    C   **G**
Jingle all the way.
C   **G**
Oh, what fun it is to ride
    D   **G**
In a one-horse open sleigh.

© Copyright 2008 Dorsey Brothers Music Limited.
All Rights Reserved. International Copyright Secured.

Verse 2

(G)
Now the ground is white,

           C
Go it while you're young,

          D
Take the girls to - night,

         G
Sing this sleighing song.

Get a bobtailed bay,

          C
Two-forty for his speed,

            D
Then hitch him to an open sleigh

            G
And you will take the lead.

Chorus 2

(G)
Jingle bells, jingle bells,

      C   **G**
Jingle all the way.

C   **G**
Oh, what fun it is to ride

     D
In a one-horse open sleigh.

    G
Oh, jingle bells, jingle bells,

      C   **G**
Jingle all the way.

C   **G**
Oh, what fun it is to ride

     D   **G**
In a one-horse open sleigh.

Lonely This Christmas

Words & Music by
Mike Chapman & Nicky Chinn

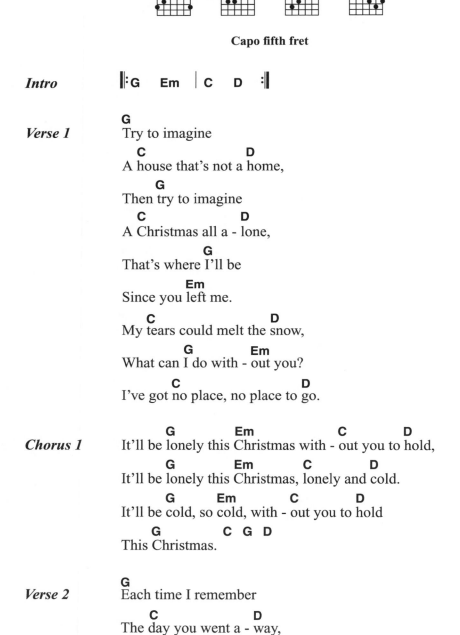

Capo fifth fret

Intro ‖: G   Em | C   D :‖

Verse 1
G
Try to imagine
   C   D
A house that's not a home,
          G
Then try to imagine
   C   D
A Christmas all a - lone,
            G
That's where I'll be
         Em
Since you left me.
     C   D
My tears could melt the snow,
          G   Em
What can I do with - out you?
     C   D
I've got no place, no place to go.

Chorus 1
          G   Em   C   D
It'll be lonely this Christmas with - out you to hold,
          G   Em   C   D
It'll be lonely this Christmas, lonely and cold.
          G   Em   C   D
It'll be cold, so cold, with - out you to hold
          G   C G D
This Christmas.

Verse 2
G
Each time I remember
   C   D
The day you went a - way,

© Copyright 1974 Chinnichap Publishing Limited.
Universal Music Publishing MGB Limited.
All Rights in Germany Administered by Musik Edition Discoton GmbH.
All Rights Reserved. International Copyright Secured.

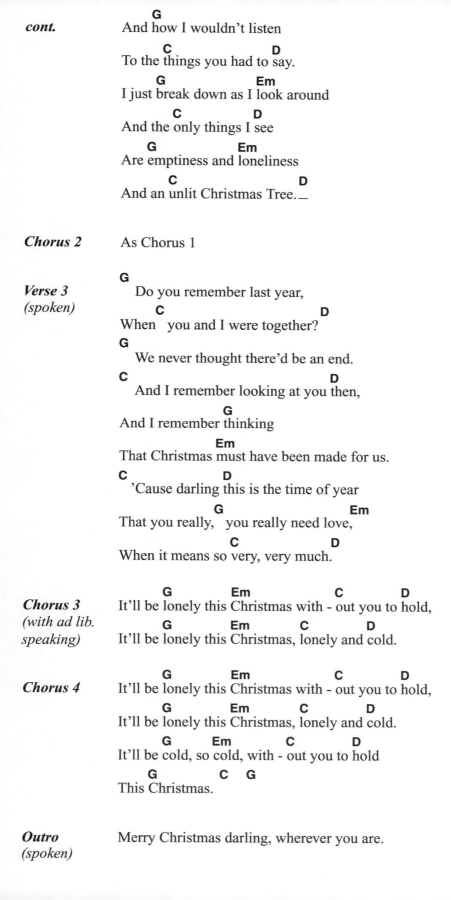

cont.

     G
And how I wouldn't listen

     C   **D**
To the things you had to say.

    G   **Em**
I just break down as I look around

     C   **D**
And the only things I see

    G   **Em**
Are emptiness and loneliness

     C   **D**
And an unlit Christmas Tree. _

Chorus 2   As Chorus 1

Verse 3   **G**
(spoken)   Do you remember last year,

     C   **D**
When you and I were together?

    G
We never thought there'd be an end.

C   **D**
And I remember looking at you then,

      G
And I remember thinking

     Em
That Christmas must have been made for us.

C   **D**
 'Cause darling this is the time of year

     G   **Em**
That you really, you really need love,

       C   **D**
When it means so very, very much.

Chorus 3   **G**   **Em**   **C**   **D**
(with ad lib. It'll be lonely this Christmas with - out you to hold,
speaking)   **G**   **Em**   **C**   **D**
It'll be lonely this Christmas, lonely and cold.

Chorus 4   **G**   **Em**   **C**   **D**
It'll be lonely this Christmas with - out you to hold,

     G   **Em**   **C**   **D**
It'll be lonely this Christmas, lonely and cold.

     G   **Em**   **C**   **D**
It'll be cold, so cold, with - out you to hold

     G   **C** **G**
This Christmas.

Outro   Merry Christmas darling, wherever you are.
(spoken)

Mary Had A Baby

Traditional

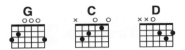

Verse 1

G   C G
Mary had a baby, oh Lord;
                      C D
Mary had a baby, oh my Lord,
G   C G
Mary had a baby, oh Lord,
            D   G
The people keep a - coming
         C   D   G
And the train done gone.

Verse 2

(G)   C G
What did she name him, oh Lord?
                    C D
What did she name him, oh my Lord?
G   C G
What did she name him, oh Lord?
           D   G
The people keep a - coming
         C   D   G
And the train done gone.

Verse 3

(G)   C G
She called him Jesus, oh Lord;
                C D
She called him Jesus, oh my Lord,
   G   C G
She called him Jesus, oh Lord,
         D   G
The people keep a - coming
        C   D   G
And the train done gone.

© Copyright 2008 Dorsey Brothers Music Limited.
All Rights Reserved. International Copyright Secured.

Verse 4

(G)   C G
Now where was he born, oh Lord?

                           C D
Now where was he born, oh my Lord?

       G   C G
Now where was he born, oh Lord?

           D   G
The people keep a - coming

         C   D   G
And the train done gone.

Verse 5

(G)   C G
Born in a stable, oh Lord,

               C D
Born in a stable, oh my Lord,

G   C G
Born in a stable, oh Lord,

         D   G
The people keep a - coming

        C   D   G
And the train done gone.

Verse 6

(G)   C G
Where did they lay Him, oh Lord?

                       C D
Where did they lay Him, oh my Lord?

G   C G
Where did they lay Him, oh Lord?

         D   G
The people keep a - coming

        C   D   G
And the train done gone.

Verse 7

```
(G)                        C  G
Laid Him in a manger, oh Lord,
                           C   D
Laid Him in a manger, oh my Lord,
G                          C  G
Laid Him in a manger, oh Lord,
              D        G
The people keep a - coming
              C    D    G
And the train done gone.
```

Verse 8

```
(G)                        C  G
Who came to see him, oh Lord?
                           C   D
Who came to see him, oh my Lord?
G                          C  G
Who came to see him, oh Lord?
              D        G
The people keep a - coming
              C    D    G
And the train done gone.
```

Verse 9

```
(G)                           C  G
Shepherds came to see him, oh Lord,
                              C   D
Shepherds came to see him, oh my Lord,
G                             C  G
Shepherds came to see him, oh Lord,
              D        G
The people keep a - coming
              C    D    G
And the train done gone.
```

Verse 10

```
(G)                              C  G
The wise men kneeled before him, oh Lord,
                                 C   D
The wise men kneeled before him, oh my Lord,
G                                C  G
The wise men kneeled before him, oh Lord,
              D        G
The people keep a - coming
              C    D    G
And the train done gone.
```

Verse 11

      (G)   **C G**
King Herod tried to find him, oh Lord,

                                 C D
King Herod tried to find him, oh my Lord,

G   **C G**
King Herod tried to find him, oh Lord,

         D   **G**
The people keep a - coming

       C   **D**   **G**
And the train done gone.

Verse 12

      (G)   **C G**
They went away to Egypt, oh Lord,

                          C D
They went away to Egypt, oh my Lord,

G   **C G**
They went away to Egypt, oh Lord,

         D   **G**
The people keep a - coming

       C   **D**   **G**
And the train done gone.

Verse 13

(G)   **C G**
Angels watching over him, oh Lord,

                            C D
Angels watching over him, oh my Lord,

G   **C G**
Angels watching over him, oh Lord,

         D   **G**
The people keep a - coming

       C   **D**   **G**
And the train done gone.

Merry Christmas Baby

Words & Music by
Lou Baxter & Johnny Moore

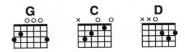

Capo second fret

Intro | G || G | C | G | C | G | C |

Verse 1

G   C
Merry Christmas baby,

      G
You sure did treat me nice.

C
Merry Christmas baby,

      G
You sure did treat me nice,

    D
You brought me a diamond ring for Christmas,

C   G | C | G | C |
I feel like I'm living in para - dise.

Verse 2

G   C
You know I'm feeling mighty fine baby,

      G
Got music on my radio.

C
I'm feeling mighty fine baby,

           G
Got some music on my radio.

D
I feel like I could kiss you baby,

C
While you're standing 'neath the mistletoe.

© Copyright 1947 St Louis Music Corporation.
Carlin Music Corporation.
All Rights Reserved. International Copyright Secured.

Instrumental | G | C | G | C ‖

| G | C | G | G | C | C | G | G |

| D | D | C | C | G | C | G | C |

Middle

G
Santa comin' down the chimney,

'Bout a half past three.

Left all them good ol' presents,

For my baby and me.

Verse 3

G   C
Merry Christmas baby,

   G
You sure did treat me nice.

D
   You brought me a diamond ring for christmas,

C   G | C | G | C |
   I feel like I'm living in para - dise.

Outro

  G   C
‖: Merry Christmas baby, Merry Christmas baby,

G   C
  Merry Christmas baby, Merry, Merry, Merry Christmas. :‖

Repeat ad lib. to fade

Once In Royal David's City

Words by Cecil Alexander
Music by Henry Gauntlett

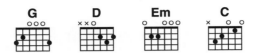

Verse 1

G   D   G   D   G
Once in   Royal David's city

Em   D   C   D G
Stood a lowly cat - tle shed.

          D   G   D   G
Where a   mother laid her baby,

Em D   C D G
In a manger for His bed.

C   G   D   G
Mary was that mother mild,

C   G   C D G
Jesus Christ her lit - tle   Child.

Verse 2

(G) D   G   D   G
He came down to earth from heaven

Em   D   C   D G
Who is God and Lord of   all,

          D   G   D   G
And His shelter was a stable,

Em   D   C   D G
And His cradle was a   stall.

C   G   D   G
With the poor and mean and lowly

C   G   C   D   G
Lived on earth our Sa - viour holy.

Verse 3

(G) D   G   D   G
And through all His wondrous childhood

Em   D   C D G
He would honour and ob - ey,

        D   G   D   G
Love and watch the lowly maiden,

Em   D   C   D G
In whose gentle arms He   lay.

C   G   D   G
Christian children all must be,

C   G   C D G
Mild, o - bedient, good as   He.

© Copyright 2008 Dorsey Brothers Music Limited.
All Rights Reserved. International Copyright Secured.

Verse 4

```
(G) D    G     D          G
For He   is our childhood's pattern,
Em       D        C D G
Day by day like us He grew,
     D    G     D       G
He was little, weak and helpless,
Em          D          C D G
Tears and smiles like us He knew,
C        G        D      G
And He feeleth for our sadness,
C        G        C D G
And He shareth in  our gladness.
```

Verse 5

```
(G) D    G      D          G
And our eyes at last shall see Him,
Em           D       C      D G
Through His own re - deem - ing love,
     D    G        D       G
For that child so dear and gentle
Em   D        C      D G
Is our Lord in heav'n a - bove,
C        G        D        G
And He leads his children on
C      G         C D G
To the place where He is   gone.
```

Verse 6

```
(G) D  G        D   G
Not in   that poor lowly stable,
Em       D   C      D G
With the oxen stand - ing by,
     D    G        D    G
We shall see Him, but in heaven,
Em   D        C      D G
Set at God's right hand on  high,
C        G        D         G
Where, like stars, His children crowned
C      G         C D G
All in white shall wait a - round.
```

Silent Night

Words by Joseph Mohr
Music by Franz Gruber

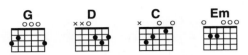

Verse 1

G
Silent night, holy night!

D   G
All is calm, all is bright.

C   G
Round yon Virgin mother and child,

C   G
Holy infant so tender and mild.

D   G   Em
Sleep in heavenly peace, —

            D   G
Sleep in heavenly peace.

Verse 2

G
Silent night, holy night,

D   G
Shepherds wake at the sight;

C   G
Glory streams from heaven afar,

C   G
Heaven hosts sing Alleluia.

D   G   Em
Christ the Saviour is born! —

            D   G
Christ the Saviour is born!

Verse 3

G
Silent night, holy night,

D   G
Son of God, love's pure light;

C   G
Radiance beams from Thy holy face,

C   G
With the dawn of redeeming grace,

D   G   Em
Jesus, Lord at Thy birth, —

            D   G
Jesus, Lord at Thy birth.

© Copyright 2008 Dorsey Brothers Music Limited.
All Rights Reserved. International Copyright Secured.

A Spaceman Came Travelling

Words & Music by
Chris de Burgh

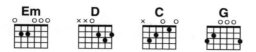

Tune guitar down by a tone

Intro | Em   D | C   Em | Em   D |

| C   D | Em | Em   ‖

Verse 1

    Em   **G**   **D**   **Em**
A spaceman came travelling on his ship from a - far,

     G   **D**   **C**
'Twas light years of time since his mission did start,

D   **Em**   **D**   **C**   **Em**
And over a village he halted his craft,

     G   **D**   **C**
And it hung in the sky like a star,

       D   **Em**
Just like a   star.

Verse 2

     (Em)   **G**   **D**   **Em**
He followed a light and came down to a shed,

     G   **D**   **C**   **D**
Where a mother and child were lying there on a bed,

Em   **D**   **C**   **Em**
A bright light of silver shone round his head,

     G   **D**   **C**
And he had the face of an angel,

          Em
And they were a - fraid.

© Copyright 1975 Big Secret Music Limited/(Renewed 1982) Rare Blue Music Incorporated.
Chrysalis Music Limited.
All Rights Reserved. International Copyright Secured.

Verse 3

       (Em)   **G**   **D**   **Em**
Then the stranger spoke, he said "Do not fear,

  G   **D**   **C**   **D**
I come from a planet a long way from here,

     Em   **D**   **C**   **Em**
And I bring a message for mankind to hear,"

G   **D**   **C**
Suddenly the sweetest music,

      D **Em**
Filled the air.

    C **D**
And it   went:

Chorus 1

Em   **D**   **C**   **Em**
La, la, la, la, la, la, la, la, la, la.

G   **D**   **C**   **D**
La, la, la, la, la, la, la.

Em   **D**   **C**   **Em**
La, la, la, la, la, la, la, la, la, la.

G   **D**   **C**
Peace and good - will to all men,

         D |**Em** |**Em** **C D** |
And love for the child.

Em   **D**   **C**   **Em**
La, la, la, la, la, la, la, la, la, la.

G   **D**   **C**   **D**
La, la, la, la, la, la, la.

Em   **D**   **C**   **Em**
La, la, la, la, la, la, la, la, la, la.

G   **D**   **C** |**Em** |**Em** |
La. _____

Verse 4

  (Em) **G**   **D**   **Em**
This lovely music went trembling through the ground,
  G   **D**   **C**   **D**
And many were wakened on hearing that sound,
  Em   **D** **C** **Em**
And travellers on the road, the village they found,
  G   **D**   **C**
By the light of that ship in the sky,
    D **Em**
Which shone all round.

Verse 5

  (Em) **G**   **D** **Em**
And just before dawn at the paling of the sky,
  G   **D**   **C**   **D**
The stranger re - turned and said "Now I must fly,
  Em   **D**   **C**   **Em**
When two thousand years of your time has gone by,
  G   **D**   **C**
This song will be - gin once a - gain,
   D **Em**
To a ba - by's cry…"
  C **D**
And it went:

Chorus 2   As Chorus 1 *Repeat ad lib. to fade*

Stay Another Day

Words & Music by
Tony Mortimer, Robert Kean & Dominic Hawken

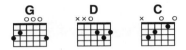

Capo seventh fret

Intro | G | D   C | G   D | C | C |

Chorus 1

G   D
          Baby if you've got to go a - way,
(Stay now…)

        C   G
Don't think I can take the pain,

             D   C
Won't you stay another day?
                 (Stay now…)

G   D
      Oh, don't leave me alone like this,

          C   G
Don't you say it's the final kiss,
               (Stay now…)

             D   C
Won't you stay another day?
                (Stay now…)

Verse 1

G   D   C
     Don't you know we've come to far now,

          G   D   C
Just to go and try to throw it all a - way.

G   D   C
     Thought I heard you say you love me,

          G   D   C
That you love was gonna be here to stay.

G   D C
     I've only just begun to know you,

          G   D   C
All I can say is won't you stay just one more day?

© Copyright 1994 Porky Publishing/Bandmodel Limited.
Universal Music Publishing Limited.
All rights in Germany administered by Universal Music Publ. GmbH.
All Rights Reserved. International Copyright Secured.

Chorus 2   As Chorus 1

                   G   D   C

Verse 2   I touch your face while you are sleep - ing,

                            G   D   C

And hold you hand, don't under - stand what's going on.

G   D   C

  Good times we had return to haunt me,

                          G   D   C

Though it's for you, all that I do seems to be wrong.

Chorus 3   As Chorus 1

                  G   D

Chorus 4   Baby if you've got to go a - way,

(Fade out   C   G

during chorus) Don't think I can take the pain,

                          D   C

Won't you stay another day?

                                (Stay now…)

                  G   D

  Oh, don't leave me alone like this,

                      C   G

Don't you say it's the final kiss,

                                (Stay now…)

                        D   C

Won't you stay another day?

                                (Stay now…)

This Is The Time

Words & Music by
Michael Bolton & Gary Burr

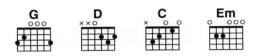

Capo ninth fret

Verse 1

    G   D
As the years say good - bye,
   C   G
One by one, on silent wings they fly.
          D
What will last, what is true,
     C   G
That's a lesson I learned loving you.
   Em   C   D   G
This world will find its way some - how,
   Em   C   D
I've got all that I need right here, right now.

Chorus 1

      G
And this is the time when the cold winds blow,

When the snow falls from heaven,
     D   C
On the dreamers be - low.
      G   D Em
And this is the time when I need to know,
     C   D
That your love will always be mine.
        C   D
Baby, this is the time,
       G
Baby this is the time.

© Copyright 1996 Mr. Bolton's Music Incorporated/Gary Burr Music Incorporated, USA.
EMI Music Publishing Limited (50%)/Universal/MCA Music Limited (50%)
(administered in Germany by Universal/MCA Music Publ. GmbH).
All Rights Reserved. International Copyright Secured.

Verse 2

          (G)   **D**
Sometimes life leads you blind,

      C   **G**
To the one that you've been waiting to find.

              D
Sometimes life lets you see,

      C   **G**
Just how great the gift of love can be.

   Em   **C**   **D**   **G**
The light that fires the brightest stars,

   Em   **C**   **D**
Is waiting to shine on this moment of ours.

Chorus 2

        G
And this is the time when the cold winds blow,

When the snow falls from heaven,

     D   **C**
On the dreamers be - low.

    G   **D**   **Em**
And this is the time when I need to know,

   C   **D**
That your love will always be mine.

          C   **D**
Baby, this is the time,

         G
Baby this is the time.

Bridge

Em   **D**
  If life is just a dream,

Em   **D**
  I know within my heart,

C   **D**
  Just getting closer to you,

C   **D**
  Is by far the sweetest part.

G   **D**
  So tell me one thing baby,

Em   **C**
  One thing I need to know.＿＿

Link | D   G | C   D |
         _____

         | G   C | D |

                                               Baby,

         G   N.C.   G

Chorus 3   This is the time when the cold winds blow,

         When the snow falls from heaven,

              D   C

         On the dreamers be - low.

            G   D   Em

         And this is the time when I need to know,

           C   D

         That your love will always be mine.

               C   D

         Baby, this is the time,

             C   D

         This is the time.

              G

         Baby, this is the time.

2 3 4 5 6 7 8 9
10/09(171517)